Chrysalis

Chrysalis

Danica Ong Teng

Life Rattle Press
Toronto

Chrysalis

Published in Canada by
Life Rattle Press
196 Crawford Street
Toronto, Ontario M6J 2V6
www.liferattle.ca

Life Rattle Press New Writers Series
ISSN 1713 8981
ISBN 978-1-989861-36-3

Cover design by Chantel Teng
Copyedited by Katherine Kurowski
Typeset by Danica Ong Teng

To my infinity four,
Thank you for always being by my side

Content Warning:

This book includes mentions of medical procedures (involving needles) and passive suicidal ideation.

Contents

Author's Note

Writing often offers release, and sometimes, a way to remember. As I try to piece these scattered memories together, words allow me to free emotions that I've been holding in and help me to remember what I went through.

Each time I write about my lupus, I discover something new from memories almost lost to fatigue and an over-medicated body. Though details fade in the past's haziness, the way I portray these events is how they live in my mind.

While revisiting some of the worst days of my life is not easy, it shows the progress I've made and strive to keep. I'm also thankful that writing my story gives me the opportunity to share my life with other people – to have them know my pain without needing to suffer through it themselves; to be reminded of the love that exists around us even if sometimes we forget.

Prologue

Do you miss the person you were before lupus?

This question broke me. It was the subject line of an email from MyLupusTeam – a lupus social network I joined a month after my diagnosis. As I stared at my screen, this question seemed to say, "you've lost something."

This thought prompted more questions. Who was I before lupus? Who am I now? And I often reflected on my answers, even long after I first thought about them.

Lupus is the "disease of a thousand faces" as its symptoms vary from person to person. I experienced my first flare and was diagnosed with lupus in August 2017 when I was eighteen years old. My symptoms – rashes, fatigue, fever, loss of appetite, and more – were at their worst, and I spent a month recovering at the Trillium Health Partners' Mississauga Hospital.

Like many people, I tiptoed around illness all my life and tried to avoid its line of sight because of the difficulties and pain it brings. We see it in people we know, we hear about it in others, we watch it in movies or read about it in books.

But the pain of disease we see from the outside can never come close to the darkness of its true depth.

After Mississauga Hospital took me in its care, I thought I would get up and start recovery right away. Get back to normal. But I didn't realize I was still falling.

My symptoms worsened, and new ones appeared.

My scalp was visible from hair loss, swollen joints were accompanied by unbearable pain, excess fluid in my lungs needed to be removed, a blackened blister on my foot grew to the size of a quarter, and I needed physiotherapy to walk again.

I continued to fall for days, stuck in that rabbit hole, never knowing if I would see light or if my story would end with me shattering on hard ground.

But after a month of medication, tests, and treatment, I was released from the hospital.

While there is treatment for lupus, there is no cure. For me, treatment means feeling stability at the cost of inhaling pills and the painful pinch of a needle every three months. But a cure would mean a life without worrying about every slight injury or when my next flare will be.

So, do I miss the person I was before lupus? Of course. I miss her so much it aches. But I'm also learning to love the one after.

A Slow Descent

My skin-cracked hand doesn't look like it belongs to an eighteen-year-old. I lie in floral blankets, propped up with fluffy pillows, and reach for the remote. Mom's queen bed faces a flat screen TV, so I'm temporarily bunking in with her. It beats my own bed's view of the wooden closet door that's falling apart.

No objections from Mom though; it's easier to watch over me this way.

I scratch with long nails at the dry flakes of skin on the back of my palm. *What else is there to watch?*

In the month I've been stuck in bed, my eyes have glazed over the titles that always show up on Netflix. I spend more time browsing through the titles than actually watching what I finally decide on. If I could walk without feeling like I rolled my ankle with each step or without the invisible weights someone *must* be putting on my back, I would run straight to a movie theatre.

Maybe even make it in time for Timeplay.

—

"It's mononucleosis," said Dr. Moore, a physician at the clinic that ran my tests.

Mononucleosis – mono for short – is an illness that can leave you with fever, fatigue, sore throat, swollen lymph nodes, sore muscles, and a loss of appetite. I felt them all.

Google says it's also known as "the Kissing Disease" as it's often transmitted through bodily fluids like saliva. *You have got to be kidding me.*

Mom shot me a look that I wondered if my boyfriend, Wilson, could feel somewhere off in the distance.

"It'll go away on its own," Dr. Moore said. "You just need to wait it out."

I trusted those words and, just like the doctor said, waited for it to go away.

—

The remote clicks when I choose a random episode of *Friends.* I've countlessly clapped along with the opening song, but it doesn't matter. Any show will do right now. I will myself to stare straight ahead at the screen and ignore the tied-up plastic bag on the floor next to me. A slight smell still escapes the bag's tight bunny ears and makes my nose twitch.

I grab the cup of water on the foldable bedside table. The cool liquid washes away the disgust in my throat. Hopefully, the water stays down. There's nothing left for my stomach to give, and it growls in anguish.

"Mom!"

My voice doesn't project as loud as I want it to, but it's enough. Soon, quick footsteps boom up the stairs, and Mom appears at the doorway. Faded brown dye flows into the tied-back waterfall of black and white hairs.

She smiles, but the worry and weariness hidden in each creased line on her face is easy to see. They've always been there, long before my lupus.

"Can you fix me miso soup, please?" I ask.

"Of course," Mom says. "Need anything else?"

"Nah, I'm good. Thanks."

"Are you sure you don't want to try eating something else?"

"I don't think I can." My arms wrap around my stomach.

"Did you throw up again?"

I nod without looking at her, staring instead at the plastic bag's tight knot.

Mom sits down next to me and gently brushes back my thin hair on one side.

"I'll bring up the soup soon." She stands up and takes the plastic bag downstairs.

Without leaving the bed, I grab another plastic bag. The bright green BTrust logo is barely legible through the crinkles. I raise it above my head and check to make sure there are no small holes at the bottom. Just in case.

To someone stuck in bed with a rebellious stomach, instant miso soup is the finest gourmet meal of powder and hot water.

The smooth burn of savoury miso soup travels down and sits warm in my stomach. The saltiness wakes my taste buds from the overload of plain water I've been drinking.

But of course, miso soup and water are not enough. So, I also drink Ensure – a meal replacement drink. Who could resist a milkshake as a meal? Especially when you're told it's healthy for you.

Soon, the pleasure of having that viscous nectar every day, often more than one bottle a day, broke the illusion. The Ensures no longer felt like a luxury but rather wet cement that I had to force down with each gulp.

But even from that first sweet sip, it wasn't a choice. I needed something to fill my stomach.

I sip spoonfuls of miso soup to make the meal last longer. Sushi would make it last longer, too. An all-you-can-eat buffet would also be nice.

My mind drifts to all the other things I want to eat. I unlock my phone, open the notepad app, and start to type.

Ramen sits at the top of my list. Pho, bubble tea, and good ol' instant noodles are close contenders. The random cravings pile up as I drag my fingers to type "Pogo" and "tacos." *What else do I want to eat when I'm better?*

I scroll down on the app to look at previous notes with similar lists. One is labelled "Wisdom Teeth" from the year before. Ramen and pho are listed here too among other foods. *Oh, that chocolate almond cake from IKEA*. Good one, me.

I daydream of the cold, layered cake touching my lips and of biting down on the sweet, crunchy combination of almonds, chocolate, and caramel. I write it down. *What else can I add?*

My spoon clinks against the bowl, and I sigh. Empty. These miso soup packets are too small.

Perfect Darkness

I keep my eyes shut and focus on the spots of light that dance around the dark abyss of my vision.

"Are you sure you wanna go in today?"

One eye opens to peer at my sister, Chantel, giving light the chance to pierce through and power the pulses in my head. Chantel sits upright beside me on the bed of KongKong and Guama's – grandpa and grandma's – guest bedroom.

Long, wavy hair falls on her face, hiding her eyes but not the concern in her voice. I close my eyes again to block out the light, but it lingers.

"Yeah, don't worry it should be fine. I'll be dropped off right in front, and I won't be there long. I already booked an appointment with the advisor. It's like going to the clinic," I say.

I dropped out of summer school after my first year at the University of Toronto Mississauga (UTM) when the fatigue started because, even though I was driven to campus, walking to my classes was a marathon.

It's nearing September, so I'm heading to UTM later to make sure things are in order for when I go back for my second year.

"I can't believe you're still planning to go to school," Chantel says.

"I really don't want to skip a year. I should feel better by the time school starts," I say.

The mono should go away soon. The doctor said it could take up to three months to completely recover, and I've been sick for about two months now.

"Still, you should be going to the hospital right now instead," Chantel says. The calm of her voice conflicts with the frustration it carries.

"Don't worry," I say. "I'll go if it's taking too long for me to feel better."

My short, disheveled black hair is visibly thinner and rests on my sunken cheeks. The bags under my eyes give the illusion that I haven't slept in days, when really, all my days now have been spent sleeping.

The only other time I've been to the hospital for sickness was years ago for stomach flu. The building was a maze. The wait times were eternal. With Mom next to me in a waiting room full of people, I spent the day heaving into a brown paper bag – another day I emptied out my stomach. I want to avoid that experience as long as I can.

Maybe Chantel's not used to seeing her little sister so pitiful. I haven't thrown an insult her way in a while.

All day I just sleep.

I pull the paper-thin bed sheets, which Guama also uses as summer blankets, around my body and close my eyes again. I try to let the darkness carry me back to sleep, but my face tightens as even sunlight is against me today.

I rest my hands over my eyes to forcibly keep them shut. But my hands drift lower to the red rashes that cover the left side of my face. I run my fingers over the bumpy terrain.

"Don't touch them," Chantel says. She smacks my hands and glares at me until she's sure I won't move them back to my face. Her gaze moves down to the rashes on my left arm. It's a minefield of red dots. "You know, even if you don't want to go to the hospital, you probably don't have much of a choice."

"What do you mean?" I say.

"I think Mom's planning to bring you to the hospital tomorrow or soon."

I guess avoiding the hospital is out. I groan at the thought of the curtained rooms, noisy machines, and desolate faces. The hospital seems too extreme for something like this if there's nothing I can do but wait.

I still need to figure out my schedule for the upcoming semester. I wrote down the courses I want to take this year, but I need to make sure the classes don't conflict so that I'm ready for enrollment time. *I'm ready.* I don't have time for the hospital.

"But I don't want to go. If we just wait it out a bit, I'm sure I'll be o-o-o-o ... It'll be fine."

Huh?

I carry on with my sentence and, with furrowed brows, turn to Chantel. But her widened eyes stare back at me and feed into my growing panic.

"Dani?" Chantel places a hand on me.

"I'm muh-muh-muh ..." But the words are trapped in my throat.

What's happening? My heart rate spikes. My mouth hangs open. My eyes cry for help.

Chantel's voice grows loud and shaky. I try to speak, but my speech only garbles. My chest tightens. My breath escapes quick and heavy.

Chantel snatches the phone from the bedside table and calls Mom. Her string of words leaves no moment to breathe.

"I'm going to call an ambulance," Chantel tells Mom. She hangs up and dials 911.

Tears blur my vision as noise outside the open window fades away. The sudden chill of Chantel's hand on my burning skin pulls my attention back to her.

"The ambulance is coming, they'll be here soon," she says. I can barely make out her words.

The oversized bells around the doorknob downstairs jingle.

"Where is she?" Mom yells from downstairs. She rushes up the steps and to my side. "Is she okay? What happened?"

"I don't know," Chantel says. "Dani was gonna say something, but she just sputtered noises. She was having trouble getting words out."

"You called the ambulance, right?" Mom asks.

"Yeah, they should be here soon."

"Okay, Guama and KongKong will be home soon too. I'll ride with Dani in the ambulance. You guys take the van and follow us there."

Minutes later, the ambulance siren blares outside. The bells jingle again. I lie in Mom's arms when two strangers appear in the room.

A woman with a blonde ponytail and a tall, buff man with dark hair wearing navy blue uniforms approach me. I can hear them shuffling around. Questions and answers go back and forth between the Uniforms and Mom. What's my name? How old am I? What happened? Do I take any medication? I slip in and out of consciousness, but I try to focus on my breathing. *In and out.* Each heavy breath keeps me here. *In and out.*

When I open my eyes again, I'm on a stretcher carried by the Uniforms. Sunshine from the skylight above the chestnut parquet stairs stab my eyes on the way down as they bring me out the door.

The bells jingle one more time as the door closes behind us.

I'm lifted through the ambulance's back double doors. The vehicle's white walls shimmer and are lined with medical equipment I can't name.

I squeeze my eyes shut for the rest of the ride. This time, the shapes of light don't dance for me. This time, I'm only left with perfect darkness.

Diagnosis

"You have lupus."

Dr. Dev's lips keep moving, but anything else he says no longer reaches me.

You have lupus.

Those three words shoot into my ear, deafening me with their sickening ring. A blank stare to match a blank mind.

The doctor's voice blends with background noise as "lupus" engraves itself into every crevice of my being. My heart races at the unknown word. *Is that bad? How bad?*

I bite the cracked skin of my bottom lip to keep me grounded.

Dr. Dev's words blur in and out of focus as rays of sunlight rest on his balding, olive head.

"An autoimmune disease …" Dr. Dev says. "… your immune system is attacking healthy tissue … no cure. Just treatment …" His eyes flick between me and Mom, but mostly Mom. "If you have any questions, just let us know."

The door closes softly behind him as he leaves room 5136 of Trillium Health Partners' Mississauga Hospital – my new room.

Mom and I stare at each other. Countless thoughts pollute the air. But none leave our lips.

I sink into the bed, letting the stiff mattress swallow me the best it can as I pull the thin white blanket closer to my face. It's not nearly as warm as my duvet at home. *Home.*

Mom sits by the window, eyes glued to her phone, as she searches up "lupus" on Google. I grab my phone too. *How did this happen to me?*

—

Lupus is a chronic autoimmune disease in which the immune system attacks its own body by damaging healthy tissues instead of only fighting foreign cells and infections.

This disease causes inflammation and a variety of other symptoms within the body, often affecting skin, joints, and internal organs.

As lupus's effect differs for each person, it is often categorized into four types.

Systemic lupus erythematosus (SLE) is the most common type among lupus patients with different levels of severity. SLE can affect major organs, causing inflammation and health complications.

The second type is cutaneous lupus erythematosus, which only affects the skin, causing rashes and sores (especially on areas exposed to sunlight).

One of the most common symptoms of lupus is the malar rash, also known as the "butterfly rash," which spreads across both cheeks and the bridge of the nose.

The third type is drug-induced lupus erythematosus, because it develops from the use of certain prescription drugs. The last type is neonatal (rare and not considered a true form of lupus), in which babies are affected by the mother's antibodies in the womb. The latter two types show similar symptoms to SLE, but most of these symptoms often disappear within months.

Lupus is not contagious, but it is possible for anyone to develop it.

Groups with a higher risk of this include women aged fifteen to forty-four, specific racial/ethnic groups, and people with a family history of lupus or any autoimmune disease. Although the trigger of lupus is not certain, many scientists factor in genetics, environment, and hormones for its development.

More information can be found on Lupus.org.

—

The more I learn about lupus, the more I piece together the past. The first sign of SLE appeared as red rashes on my face, but not the telltale butterfly rash as it was only on my left cheek.

The lumpy red dots made their way down my body, painting the length of my left arm. Fatigue followed soon after.

Even now, I can barely do anything. I run out of breath after a few steps. I drift off just to wake up and go back to sleep. Cycling in endless darkness.

Three doctors diagnosed my problems as mononucleosis and said it would go away on its own.

But I should've known something was wrong when my symptoms worsened.

For more than a month I was bedridden and barely ate, waiting for the pains to go away on their own, because I believed it was mono. But it's not mono. And it took over a week of hell just to figure out it was lupus.

Maybe a butterfly could've saved me a lot of suffering.

Dark thoughts take root in my mind and fester. They won't go away. Just like the lupus won't go away.

Mom squeezes next to me on the narrow hospital bed.

"Don't worry, it's going to be fine," she says.

"I know ..." I say. "I'll be okay."

She hugs me tight and kisses my forehead.

Who knows if we both believe it at the moment, but it's what we want to believe.

Pin Cushion

I'm not sure if I'll ever get used to the prick of a needle, or the anxiety that builds the moment before the needle tip breaches flesh.

The first two weeks at the hospital have littered my body with pinpricks. All the punctures mark tests ordered by doctors when they were trying to figure out my diagnosis. Now, to control my lupus, they need to constantly monitor my blood levels.

Each day, the nurses continue to come for blood tests. Each day, I wonder if it'll be quick and painless, or long and slow. It's a game of chance for someone like me, whose veins are small and hard to find.

A knock at the door signals the nurse who's here to draw my blood. I let out a deep breath and try to relax. *In and out.* That's what the nurses tell me to do when the blood doesn't come out.

"Come in," I say.

"Hello, my name is Gabi," the nurse says. She wheels in a metal cart topped with medical supplies and closes the door behind her. "I'm here to do your bloodwork for today."

"Hi," I say. My voice comes out much quieter than I intended.

Mom gets up to greet Gabi as well and continues to watch us instead of going back on her phone.

"Okay, let's see here." Gabi's eyes move down a paper as she mumbles to herself what tests she needs the blood for.

She tries to start a conversation, but I only manage short responses and some nods as I glue my eyes to the swift movements of her hands. As the nurse talks, she brings out a handful of empty vials with different coloured caps and labels them.

"Show me your arm, please," Gabi says.

I stretch out my left arm to show her a dark purple bruise just above my inner forearm.

"Oh, how about the other arm? It might be painful if we do it on this one," she says.

"Uh, it's okay. Because my other arm is …"

I show her my right arm, revealing even more bruises.

"Oh, honey," she says. She frowns as she holds my arms and examines them. "Okay, let's stick with the left one then."

I lay my arm flat in front of her, and she ties a blue band tight around my upper arm. She tells me to make a tight fist, but my hands are too weak, so I bury my nails into my palm to keep a fist formed.

Gabi holds my arm in one hand and uses the other to press along its length with her index finger, checking for viable spots from which to draw blood.

Her brows furrow, and I know I'm in trouble. After bouncing her finger on one spot a couple of times, she rubs it down with alcohol.

Deep breaths. *In and out.*

She takes the needle out of its packaging. *In and out.*

"Take a deep breath, honey," she says. *Believe me, I am trying.*

I turn my head away and close my eyes as she brings the long, thin needle close to my arm. In the next second, a sharp pain penetrates my skin. *Please. Please let there be blood.*

I open my eyes and turn to look.

The needle is embedded in my skin, but the connecting tube and vials are empty. My stomach sinks at the sight. *Okay, it's fine. Try again. A different spot. Just please don't –*

But Gabi isn't a mind reader.

Before I can say anything, she fishes, pushing the needle in deeper. I wince and squeeze my eyes shut again.

One eye opens to peek, but still nothing.

Click! I bite down hard on my lip as the needle retracts.

"Sorry," Gabi says. "Your veins are so tiny. We'll try a different spot."

I muster only a nod. The process repeats. The second needle goes in and hurts more than the first. I look. Still no blood. She begins to fish again, and I feel the needle move in. My eyes sting. I exhale. *In and out.* The needle retracts.

Gabi exhales through her nose. She looks at my arm and covers the needle marks with a cotton ball.

"Sorry, hon. Press down on that for now. I'll be back, I'm going to call another nurse."

I nod. When Gabi leaves the room, Mom comes up to me and holds my hand.

"Are you alright? Does it hurt?" Mom says.

Again, I nod. My teeth sink further into my pale lips, cracking the layer of dry skin. My nose flares as I try not to cry, but the glossiness of my eyes gives me away.

Mom clenches her teeth and shakes her head. Her grip on my hand tightens.

Another nurse comes in my room, while Gabi follows close behind and explains that she's having trouble.

"Hi, you must be Danica. My name is Ava," the new nurse says. "I hear your veins are quite hard to find. Let's take a look."

I try to smile at her but don't say anything. I think I'll cry if I open my mouth right now.

I give her my left arm, and she presses her finger down on multiple spots. Her head tilts back and forth, trying to get a good angle. But it's no good.

She takes my right arm and does the same. After a few moments, she settles on a spot amid the splash of bruises. She prepares my arm for the needle, tells me to breathe, and sinks it in. My face twists as the pain intensifies.

I look to the vials. Empty. She digs deeper.

"How are you doing?" Ava asks, keeping her eyes on the needle.

Instead of words, my mouth lets out only a whimper. Everyone turns to look at me, and the sobs break free. The needle retracts, and they all try to calm me down, but I can't. I just can't.

Stop. Please just let it stop.

The nurses still need to draw blood, but I'm still wailing as they figure out the best way to do it. They try my right arm again. The needle digs in deeper and deeper, desperate for blood. My inner arm burns. I can feel the tip slither underneath my skin. I cry out as I feel nothing but searing pain.

On the next try, the nurses finally draw blood from a spot on the back of my left hand. A painful spot. It's already over, but I'm still crying.

Needles in my arms. Needles in my hands. Needles in my back. Needles in my stomach.

Long after the nurses leave, I look at the holes in my arm. Dark blotches tinged with purple and yellow cover a third of my left forearm. Vibrant, plum-coloured patches pigment the surface of the skin on my right arm.

I must look like a pin cushion to them.

Round and Round

Morning

Sun shines through the large window that lines the wall of room 5136 at Mississauga Hospital. I blink twice and wipe the sleepiness from my eyes. A third, hard blink accepts my surroundings as reality, and the ache of waking up in this room that's not my own sets in for another day.

I look to the side where Mom sleeps on a chair that pulls out to become a bed. She falls asleep fast, but I wish I could offer her my bed instead.

She refuses to go home while I'm here.

My gaze fixes on the clock – almost 9:00 a.m. The hospital staff will be coming in soon to bring my breakfast. I lie still in the meantime and listen to the hum of machinery around me. Outside my room, the muffled movements and voices of doctors, nurses, patients, and visitors fill the hallway.

Even in the early morning, people bustle about. At home, on the days when I don't sleep past noon like usual, I'm used to the quieter calm of mornings.

But no matter what time it is here, the hospital is awake twenty-four seven. Illness, injury, and death act on their own time.

I close my eyes again and try to stretch out the remaining minutes before my hospital routine starts. The machines hum me a lullaby, drifting me back to sleep.

Knock knock knock. The noise startles me awake. I look at Mom as she sits up in her chair.

A woman with brown hair tied up in a ponytail enters my room holding a tray of food. She places it down on a wooden table by the door and wheels it over to me. We exchange morning greetings, then my eyes follow the woman's ponytail as it bounces out the door.

My fingers trace over everything on the tray: a cup of water, a tuna salad sandwich, a mug of black tea, sugar and cream packets, a mini carton of milk, and a bottle of Ensure. I glare at the bottle, which I've been drinking almost every day for the past two months. On the corner of the tray, a mini paper cup holds a variety of colourful pills.

"Hey." Mom shakes her finger at me. "Brush your teeth first."

"Yeah, of course. I know," I say.

In and out. I take a deep breath and groan as Mom helps me up. My legs peek out first and hang over the bed. She clutches my arms and steadily helps me into the wheelchair. I roll into the washroom and reach for my toothbrush.

The few minutes it takes to wash up leaves me out of breath. I go back to bed. My shoulders slump down, and my head buries into the pillow. *Can I just rest here for the whole day?*

Mom pulls the wooden table over the bed so that everything is spread out in front of me. I open Netflix on my phone and set up *How to Get Away with Murder.* The show plays as I munch on my sandwich. I tear open the sugar and cream packets and dump them in my hot tea. The dark liquid turns light brown as I stir up a whirlpool with my spoon.

I've always been a slow eater, so it takes a while to finish my breakfast. But the Ensure takes the longest. Each gulp of the creamy liquid makes me gag.

"It's only a small bottle," Mom says.

"I can't do it," I say.

My lips turn inward each time the sickly sweet smell comes close. I pinch my nose and turn what would have been three large gulps into a dramatic three-act play. Once it's finished, I move onto the sequel: the medicine.

I grab the cup of water and take my pills: propranolol, prednisone, spironolactone, hydroxychloroquine, iron, calcium, and vitamin D.

I start with the smallest ones and work my way up. But even the small ones seem like a choking hazard. My hand reaches for the circular, dark green propranolol, which lowers my heart rate.

Chantel said that when I arrived at the hospital in the ambulance, my heart rate was at around 180 beats per minute. Normal resting heart rates are around sixty to one hundred.

I force the rest of the pills down one at a time, wishing all medication came in the form of multivitamin gummy bears instead.

My nurse for the day, Emilia, knocks and enters my room to check my vital signs.

Another older nurse, Hazel, comes in next to give me my blood thinner shot for the day. As bad as pills are, needles are far worse.

"Where did you have the shot last time?" Hazel asks as she readies the needle.

"On the left side," I say.

I lift my shirt until just below my chest and brace myself for a prick on the right side of my stomach. I suck in air through my teeth as the needle sticks out in a split second, leaving a tiny red mark in its place.

"Sorry, sweetie," she says as she sees me wince. "All done."

Hazel places a Band-Aid over the puncture, and Emilia lays a heated blanket over me.

"Thank you," I say. I lower my shirt and place my hands over my stomach where the needle pierced.

Resting my hands there doesn't do anything, but in my mind, it helps ease the pain.

Afternoon

The bustle outside my room grows with time as more visitors flood the hospital, but I'm too engrossed in my show to care. For someone who spends most of their time in bed, there's not much else to do.

A loud knock at the door interrupts the endless stream of episodes.

A woman brings in a tray that almost mirrors breakfast's, except this time, instead of a sandwich, it's a plate of pasta, and instead of milk, it's apple juice.

And more pills, of course.

As I get started with lunch, a different staff member comes in and takes my meal order for the next day.

"Chicken salad sandwich or macaroni and cheese?" she asks.

"Macaroni and cheese, please," I say.

"Apple juice or orange juice?"

"Apple juice, please."

"Green tea or black tea?"

I think I'll make milk tea tomorrow.

"Black tea, please."

I thank her as she takes down the rest of my order and leaves the room.

Once lunch is done, and the clock hits 3:30 p.m., Annie enters my room to help me with physiotherapy.

"Hey, you ready?" Annie says.

"Yup, sorry. Give me one sec." I put down my phone and push the table away.

"No worries, take your time."

Annie brushes back her short, chestnut hair to show a smile and pushes up her lilac-rimmed glasses.

Both Mom and Annie support me as I get up from bed. Annie places a walker in front of me, and I lean all my weight on it just to stand. My legs wobble, with each violent shake reminding me that I would crumble without this walker.

With slow steps we exit the room, except for Mom, who stays. The door doesn't lock, and Mom worries about leaving our stuff unattended.

I take on today's physio goal step by step with Annie at my side. The goal used to be from my bed to the wheelchair. Then from wheelchair to walker. Now, we'll usually try to circle the fifth floor at least once.

"How are you feeling today?" Annie asks.

"I'm okay, could be better though," I say. Gloom clings to my laugh. "I hate needing this thing to walk."

I look down at my crusty hands on the walker. *Pathetic.* No chance of dance practices anytime soon. I can't even stand on my own. Hell, I can't do anything on my own. This body doesn't feel like it's mine.

"Don't worry, you're already making great progress. Soon, you won't even need that walker," Annie says.

"I hope so."

The looming hallway stretches ahead of me. The never-ending path feels like a taunt, convincing me that I'm trapped within its uniform walls. We're only halfway across the whole floor, but the hospital's cold, tiled ground starts to look like the softest bed.

"Do you need to take a break?" Annie says.

"No, I'm okay," I say.

My clenched teeth are hidden behind that lie. I want to make it back to my room with no stops. *I have to.*

We finally loop back around to room 5136 where Mom and Annie help place me back on the bed. I pant and hope they're too distracted with their conversation to notice my quick breaths. *In and out.*

"Good job today," Annie says to me. "I'll see you again tomorrow."

"Thanks, and yup, see you tomorrow," I say.

The door closes softly behind her.

Sweat sticks all over my body, but I don't want to leave my bed again. I don't feel like watching Netflix. I don't feel like doing anything, so I fall asleep and don't wake up until dinner arrives at my door.

Night

Through the window, I watch as the rest of the day passes. The glass shows a dark shade of blue, telling me another day is almost over and that hopefully I'm one day closer to going home.

After the last tray of food and pills for the night, I struggle into a different kind of wheelchair: a shower commode. Mom helps me undress and wheels me in. She turns on the water and holds the nozzle away, testing the temperature first with her hand.

"Here, I can do it." I reach for the nozzle, but Mom pulls away.

"It's okay, just let me do it for now," she says.

Soothing warm water falls over me, soaking my head and body. A clump of hair falls with the water and swirls around the drain.

I comb my hands through my dark hair, and more strands fall out. Too many at a time. I let out a shaky breath, but my face remains still.

Each fallen strand leaves me emptier. I sit on the commode like a limp doll as Mom continues to wash my body for me. My eyes fixate on the drain. Dark strands float round and round.

Tomorrow will be the same.

Just Breathe

"I need to get out of here!"

My words are unrecognizable through the cries that break out. I hunch over on the hospital bed with my legs tucked in. I clench the rough, white blanket in my fists and squeeze my eyes shut until my entire face burns.

Mom tries to calm me down, but my sobs drown out her voice. She tries to hold me, but I push her away. *Stop, just stop.*

The room around me spins – the same squeaky sink that never shuts up, the same window with the one-star view of the parking lot, the same maddening hum of machinery around me. The same fucking scene over and over again that won't be satisfied until it suffocates me.

The only things that ever change around here are the date and the nurse's name written on the whiteboard in front of my bed.

"I'll take care of this," Chantel says, grabbing my arm. "Dani needs to get out of this room."

"No, I don't wanna get up," I whine, pushing her arm away.

"Get up, now." Chantel grabs my arm again, this time with a firm grip, and supports me so I stand. "We're taking a walk."

Chantel leads me to the door, and Mom doesn't try to follow. I struggle to stifle my cries until finally, they settle to violent sniffles.

The moment I leave the room, my head clears and brings everything back into focus. The open hallway feels less stuffy, and I can breathe again.

Chantel leads me to the nearby seating area amid the elevators and large glass windows. She helps lower me onto one of the small, cushioned seats arranged in a semicircle. Two middle-aged nurses on their break sit in front of me, and an older janitor rests on the chair beside.

I look down at my lap, but I can feel their eyes on me. I don't blame them. I might stare too. My hair looks like a hay bale, my bright green pajama pants with purple cartoon cats don't match my turquoise top, and my constant sniffles and sobs sound like an engine sputter.

"Here eat this." Chantel takes out a clementine and digs her nails into the soft peel. She places a small segment in my hand.

"I can't do this anymore …" I say. I fixate my gaze on the clementine piece in my palms, tracing over the fruit's intricate lines. Each sniffle carries in the smell of citrus. "I can't go back to that room."

When I picture that room, I'm right back in the bed surrounded by boring, beige walls. I wake up, have breakfast, eat pills, get a blood thinner shot, eat lunch, more pills, physiotherapy, dinner, more pills, and all the time in between is spent either in bed or in a room where the doctors run tests. MRIs, CT scans, X-rays, ultrasounds, IVs, blood tests, and more that I can't even remember in my drowsiness.

My shoulders slump. I can feel the tears build up again behind closed eyes. Unable to suppress them, they slide down my cheeks.

That room has kept both my mind and body prisoner for weeks now, leaving me drained. Sometimes, I'm let outside in a wheelchair to get fresh air, and again I'm reminded of how suffocating the inside really is.

Fresh air becomes a nostalgic memory that I forget after too long in that room, and it only returns when I inhale the cool breeze and feel the sun's warmth on my skin. My heart hurts because

I crave it desperately, but then I remember that I need to hide from the sun because lupus has made me photosensitive and that the effort to go outside takes too much of a toll on my body.

The window in my room is my only view of the outside, but that same scene of cars driving in and out of the parking lot is now infuriating.

"Let's just stay out here for now," Chantel says. "As long as you want."

"I just want to leave. When can I leave already?" I say. My voice fades into a mumble, unsure if I want Chantel to hear me or not.

I look toward the hall we came from and dread going back to the room. I miss my white walls full of posters and polaroid pictures at home. I miss the giant stuffed panda that rests on my bed. I miss my shelves of books that I haven't opened since middle school.

"I don't know how much longer I can take this," I say.

I turn my head to the crowd of people that pass by. Each with different reasons to be here, with their own stories, but all surrounded by sickness. Janitors travel the halls with carts of sanitizer. Visitors are either lost or on a clear path to a room they've visited before. Elderly patients chat with their nurses.

Everyone on this floor is much older than me.

My head pulses, drumming louder by the second. I ball my hands into fists, and my nails leave deep crescents in my palms.

Thinking about my useless body unlocks a feral anger within me, and each passing thought redirects my rage to anything I can think of – people who take their health for granted, the doctors who misdiagnosed me with mono, and myself most of all.

I should be thankful I'm not dead.

But sometimes, it doesn't seem that way. And sometimes, my mind fiddles with the idea of crossing a dangerous line. A one-way ticket. But that terrifies me beyond my own comprehension.

I shake my head and brush away the thought, but it tends to sneak back in during sleepless nights. The thought that it would be so simple to simply not exist.

Lupus attacks me physically, but it seems I'm perfectly capable of destroying myself mentally.

"If I stay here any longer, I swear I'm gonna go crazy," I say with a sniffle.

Chantel lets out a deep sigh and puts more clementine pieces in my hand.

"You'll be okay," Chantel says. "It shouldn't be too much longer. You'll be out soon. Just breathe."

Her words calm me, and I focus on each breath. *In and out.* I rub my eyes dry with my free hand and pop the clementine pieces in my mouth with the other. The sweet taste lingers.

"Thanks, Chant," I say.

"Don't worry about it."

We stay there together and finish the clementine in silence.

I stare out the windows. It's the same parking lot that's visible from my room. But from another angle, it looks different here.

I guess that's something new.

A Day Like Home

Three, two, one …

"Happy birthday!"

Mom and Chantel hug me the moment the clock hits midnight. Whether at home or in the hospital, our birthday tradition of midnight greetings hasn't changed.

I sit up in bed and try to wrap my arms around them. Our voices interrupt the quiet evening in our little room, though we tone it down to match the machines' subtle drone.

We don't want to bother the other patients, especially those who are already asleep. When you know you're not home, the night can stretch every second, numbing your mind and eyes until you see the first lights of sunrise.

"Thank you," I say. "Didn't think I'd be spending my birthday in the hospital this year."

"Probably not," Chantel says. "But hopefully the cake tomorrow will help."

"Be careful on your way back from the mall," Mom says. "Let's go to sleep. Chant, you need to sleep early so you're not tired at work in the morning."

"Yeah, don't worry, I'll be fine. I'll text when I'm on my way to the hospital," Chantel says.

I lean back down until my head rests against the pillow and pull the blanket over my shoulders. Mom takes the regular chair for tonight and tells Chantel to use the sleeper chair so she's well-rested for work. I curl my legs up and hug my body. My bed is too small for two people.

There was a stretcher that Mom used as a bed in here before, but one night, she had an unsettling nightmare of a man's silhouette. The next morning, she asked the nurses for help to take it out.

The outlines of furniture around the room sharpen as my eyes adjust to the darkness. It feels useless for me to have the bed while I'm still wide awake.

The torment of feeling tired but being unable to sleep is maddening. The night's darkness unleashes Pandora's box. And that's more terrifying than any ghost. Dread and despair rip me open from the inside. Every unspeakable secret that I've worked so hard to bury comes out in show-and-tell. The ones that reveal every anxiety about the future. The ones that say I'm unloved or unworthy of love. The ones that strip away at my self-esteem.

And the ones that fear my own mortality but are tempted to welcome it.

Without realizing, I manage to pass out and wake up when sunlight infiltrates my eyelids.

At 9:00 a.m., I receive my first birthday present: breakfast with a side of pills. Whole wheat bread with margarine, a cup of black tea, sugar and cream packets, a miniature box of Rice Krispies cereal, a small carton of milk, and a bottle of Ensure rest on the dark green tray. The paper cup of colourful pills sits in the corner. The usual breakfast.

The paper that shows my food order and name also has *Happy Birthday Danica!* printed on it with a smiley face drawn in yellow highlighter.

I start by forcing down the dry bread of the sandwich. I take the lid off the cup and peer down at it. Murky, hot tea swishes around with floating flecks of some unidentified substance. My lips turn in as I put the cup down and cover it again. *I guess I'm not having hospital-version milk tea today.*

Even the cup itself reminds me of the ones you see in prison on TV, clanging against the metal bars of the cell. Except my cell is deceiving in comparison – pleasantly decorated with big beige walls, bright flowers, as well as a wide, unopenable window that gives the illusion of freedom.

The nurse returns to bring me water to take with my pills. I smile at the Styrofoam cup etched with drawings done in pink pen of confetti, balloons, a stick figure with a party hat, a two-tier cake with candles, and the words *Happy Birthday Danica!* in the middle. On top reads *Have an amazing birthday!*

While spending my birthday in the hospital is far from amazing, I hold the cup tight and chuckle.

The last thing left on my tray is the bottle of Ensure. What a surprise.

"Why do I still need this?" I say. I pick up the bottle and toss it between my hands to prolong the inevitable.

"You need to gain more weight," Mom says.

"Aren't I doing that already with the food they're giving me?"

"It's not enough, you still need more."

Even before I was malnourished, Mom would sometimes tell me that I should gain more weight. After I ended up below one hundred pounds during my bedridden days at home, I was more inclined to believe her.

The sight of the blue and white bottle with the image of a delicious vanilla milkshake makes me sigh. The grooves of the bottle cap dig into my hand as I reluctantly twist it open. I close my eyes and clip my nostrils shut with my fingers in preparation for the first sip.

The creamy liquid is thick and cool. I know if I let go of my nose for even a second, the artificial taste of vanilla will scream at me. Every part of my body wants to reject it as soon as it slides to the tip of my tongue. My face distorts in disgust, and I pull away.

I look to Mom, eyes pleading for help, but she only gives me a glare that says *you better finish every last drop*. How is it possible for a bottle that fits in the palm of my hand to seem so bottomless? I pinch my nostrils again and chug the rest of the drink.

"I have some news that'll make your day better," Mom says.

"What?" I say. I stick my tongue out, still trying to get rid of the taste of Ensure.

"When everyone comes later to celebrate, they're also bringing some takeout food for us. The usual Chinese party trays. Chantel's bringing cake."

My face lights up at the mention of Chinese food. On birthdays, we usually order party trays from a Chinese restaurant: some chicken wings, maybe beef with black bean sauce, but always Cantonese chow mien. Even if they're not specifically chow mien, noodles are always a staple on birthdays as Mom says they represent long life.

Outside the window, the sky darkens to a deep blue. People knock and enter – KongKong, Guama, Chantel, and Wilson cram into the hospital room with me and Mom. I sit up in the bed with everyone surrounding me.

"Hi, KongKong. Hi, Guama," I say. They hug me tight and wish me happy birthday.

Even if they don't come inside all the time, they've been driving to the hospital almost every day to bring food and check up on me. KongKong asks me how I'm doing and tells me about the latest technology. Guama asks me if I've been eating enough and reminds me to pray.

Their faces haven't changed much for me, but I'm sure I've changed for them – from baby, to toddler, to teen, to a thin resemblance of who I used to be, stuck in a hospital bed.

"Happy birthday, love," Wilson says. He comes up to me next and kisses me on the head.

"Thanks for coming," I say. "I'm glad you're here."

My brother, Justin, gets a pass for not being here because he's in Japan. We didn't give him too many details about how sick I got. I'm out of danger, and he's coming home in a few days, so there's no point in making him worry on the way back.

After all the trays are laid out on the tiny table, Mom assembles food on a plate and hands it to me.

My eyes eat first. The long chow mien noodles shine with sauce so slippery you can hear it as they swirl through the chopsticks; bright green broccoli, soft pink shrimps, and other meats hide like gems among the waves of yellow noodles. The chicken wings drip with oil, and the crispy skin cracks under the weight of my fingers. The aroma of beef in black bean sauce goes straight to my mouth; it doesn't lie to you – the beef tastes just as savoury as it smells.

These are not the healthiest foods, but it's a nice break from what I've been eating. Hospital foods always taste the same even though they're different dishes – they're foods to satisfy basic survival needs rather than pleasure the taste buds.

"Take a bite first," Mom says.

"Whoops," I say. My fingers maneuver the chopsticks and slip a bite of noodles into my mouth mid-laugh. It's tradition to let the birthday person take the first bite before anyone else can eat.

When sauce residue and clean chicken bones are the only remains on everyone's plates, Mom pulls out the cake. But it's not just any cake, it's chocolate mousse cake from Akko Cake House, another familiar treat. The hospital staff doesn't allow lit candles inside, so with the bright lights on above, Mom places the cake in front of me and everyone begins to sing "Happy Birthday."

Everything, even the excessive oil from the takeouts, reminds me of home. It's a fleeting familiarity that I want to hold on to. I squeeze Wilson's hand as I look around at everyone. They all smile at me.

Even though we can't light the candles on the cake, I make a wish anyways.

Far Away

Dude, where are you?

My long fingernails clack against the phone screen as I type.

Once I was feeling a bit better, the hospital allowed more visitors to come see me. I didn't realize how lonely I was until I saw familiar faces other than Mom and Chantel.

Ding! A new message from my friend Chris pops up.

I'm here … but I can't find the room?? Are you sure you gave me the right room number?

I tilt my head upward in thought. I've been in this room for weeks, of course I know the room number.

I roll my eyes and text Chris again.

LOL yes of course! Room 3156. Just ask someone, the staff or something.

Mom sits by the window on the sleeper chair. She wears reading glasses and focuses on her phone, scrolling through motivational and informational posts shared by relatives in our family Viber group chat.

Ding! Chris replies, *I did. They said they don't have that room and told me to ask you for the room number again.*

I sigh, fingers ready to respond. The whiteboard in front of my bed catches my eye before I type. Letters are scratched off, but scrawled in marker I read:

Room 5136
Nurs : Hanna
Today s: Fri, Sep 8 2017
Goal for today: Blood Test

I squint at the tiny black text in the corner – Room 5136. Just like the cellphone service in this hospital, the signal from my eyes to my brain is delayed. *Ding!* My head shoots up from its tilted position. *Oh shit, he's gonna kill me.*

I hurry to text Chris the correct room number, and a few minutes later, there's a knock at the door.

"Come in," I say.

Chris's lanky figure appears in the doorway. He wears a zip-up hoodie as always. His tousled black hair moves side to side as he shakes his head. He crosses his arms and glares, but he can't help but laugh as well.

"Hey, Chris. Errr … took you long enough," I say.

"Are you kidding me," he says. "I knew it was the wrong room number!"

"Sorry sorry," I say, but I can't stop laughing. "I really thought it was 3156. I must've mixed up the numbers."

He flares his nostrils and puts both hands to his forehead.

"Danica! Oh, my god. They told me that room didn't exist. They looked at me like I was crazy!"

"Hey, you can't blame me," I say. "I'm still a bit loopy from all the meds I'm taking."

I'm not out of the hospital yet, but I'm already learning to play my lupus like a get-out-of-jail-free card.

Mom greets Chris, and after chatting for a bit, she leaves the room. Chris pushes the cushioned chair from out of the corner, turns it to face me, and plops down in the seat.

"So, how are you doing?" he says.

"I'm okay." I give a faint smile. "Well, I mean, definitely could be better. I guess."

We swap stories and update each other on our lives since high school days. It's been about a year since I've seen any of my friends at our last get-together.

"That reminds me, thanks for writing in my birthday card," I say.

"Of course, no worries."

On my birthday, Wilson gave me a customized card with a corgi's butt on the front. The card was filled with messages he collected from friends I haven't seen in a while. It was perfect inside and out. He knows that he can win my heart with a corgi butt.

A few other friends have visited too. I wish I could see them more often, but I know everyone's busy preparing to go back to school. I would've been doing the same.

Most of my friends attend universities in different cities, so these are the last few days I can see anyone for a long time.

The card sits by the window with colourful balloons and other birthday gifts that friends and family left for me: a tiny pumpkin and a succulent, a book of writing prompts and a set of pens, a bright pink Build-A-Bear with a "Get Well Soon" shirt, a glass dome with string lights, a pink unicorn plush, a hand fan from a concert I had to miss, and bouquets of flowers.

Chris keeps me company for a couple of hours, then it's time for him to go too. I thank him for visiting, and we say our goodbyes.

Mom returns to the room, and I slouch back into my pillow. I turn onto my side and hug my legs. Looks like university will have to wait. I dread the start of school every year, but this time, I would've gladly welcomed it. I'm going to have to graduate a year later now, without most of my friends.

Problems buzz in my head one after the other. My eyes flicker as I try to fight off the oncoming drowsiness, but soon, I cave into my exhaustion.

I open my eyes slowly, waiting for them to adjust to the light. Chantel's here now and rests on the sleeper chair. Mom sits in the other chair, scrolling through her phone. They look up at me when I sit straight in my bed, stretching and yawning.

"Hey, can you bring the table here, please?" I ask Mom. My hands grab air, like a baby reaching for its toy.

Mom stands from her chair, and she wheels the table to hover over the bed and in front of me. My MacBook, with its cyan case covered in Pokémon and panda stickers, rests on top of the wooden surface.

"Not too close," Mom says. She points at the screen as I open the laptop. "Your eyes."

I nod without looking at her, my eyes already fixated on the glowing screen. I open Google Chrome and click the Facebook bookmark at the top. One message notification from my friend Melissa appears.

Danica, we made you a video! I really wish we could get more people to participate but filming one's self is actually really hard. Hope you enjoy!

Attached to the message is a YouTube link. The video is titled "We Love You Danica!" and plays a compilation of video messages from her and some of my other friends: April, Jordine, Emily, Kristen, Celine, and Melody.

Within three seconds, my eyes sting. In the next, one blink sets all the tears loose.

For three minutes and fifteen seconds, I watch as my friends tell me that they miss me and that they love me from their residences in different cities. They catch me up on their lives and wish me to get well soon, as "Rhythm of Love" by Plain White T's plays in the background.

Mom and Chantel rush to see what's going on when they hear me bawling. They bring me the tissue box and rub my back. I pull out tissue after tissue. The tears blur my vision, and I can't control the volume of my sobs as they drown out the video. I raise the volume. I don't care if people in the hall hear my cries.

After the video ends, I play it again.

My hands stay close to my face like windshield wipers as they sweep the rain away from my eyes. Tissues pile around me. I sit hunched and clutch the collar of my shirt. It's a rainstorm now.

Going Home

September 26, 2017

One month ago, on this same day, I was admitted to Trillium Health Partners' Mississauga Hospital.

Today, I'm leaving.

Mom asked when I could go home, and Dr. Dev gave her a choice. I was cleared to go home if that's what we wanted. But if we were still concerned, he could transfer me to a semi-private room in a different ward to keep monitoring me.

Mom's intuition told her I needed to go home; she would listen to it this time.

She still regrets not taking me to the hospital sooner at the beginning because she had trusted the three different medical professionals who told her it was mono.

I think back to the beginning. My first week at the hospital still remains hazy to me; all I remember is the pain of multiple procedures.

But Mom's voice quivers whenever she recalls what I can't remember. She often tells me about the time I had a seizure when my diagnosis was still unknown. Her haunting cries echoed through the halls as she screamed for help.

She couldn't handle the thought that I could be here one second and gone the next.

Now, I wait in my hospital room and sit in the large, cushioned chair by the window. I've grown so thin that I feel like Goldilocks in Papa Bear's chair.

Mom talks to the nurses as they go over my discharge papers. KongKong and Guama are on their way to pick us up in their minivan. Everyone decided it was best for me to stay at their house for a while. It's closer to both Mom's workplace and the Mississauga Hospital in case there's an emergency. It also means there's always someone home to take care of me.

Looking around the room, I remember how trapped I felt just a week ago.

I stare at the bed to my left. The bed I've slept in for a month. The white blanket is crumpled in a ball at the bottom, making the single blue pillow look lonely at the opposite end of the plain bedsheet.

The buttons on the side that adjust the angle of the entire top half is the only improvement I would make to my own bed at home.

There's not much left to pack now because Chantel brought some stuff home ahead of time.

On the wooden table in front of me are my wilting flowers that Mom temporarily placed in water bottles. I use the Styrofoam cups that I've kept from my birthday as pots to hold them for extra support. They take up two spots in an old Tim Hortons cup holder.

Beside them, four balloons held down by a weight are running out of breath.

I check the time on my phone – 4:18 p.m. I click the lock button, and the black screen shows my reflection.

My front hair is pulled back, exposing an empty hairline. The rest of the thin black strands curls up around my shoulders. My lips are pale, but the rashes on my face are gone. The hairs on my brows are sparse, making it look like I have none. *Okay, fine, that one I can't blame on the lupus.* It's always been like that.

Mom returns to the room and hands me papers that tell me everything I need to do once I'm home.

"I asked the hospital staff if they could send people to check up on you for a few weeks," Mom says. "There's going to be a nurse that will come once every week to clean the wound on your foot and a physiotherapist on a different day to help you with your exercise."

The side of my foot is still bandaged from when a doctor popped the blister caused by my bedridden days. I had cried from the pain. The blister left behind two circular wounds surrounded by ripped skin, making it look like a pig's nose.

"Sounds good," I say. My foot taps the floor. I run my thumb under the hospital identification band on my wrist. "Are KongKong and Guama almost here?"

"Almost. We should probably head to the entrance now," Mom says.

Mom lets the nurses know we're leaving, and they help me into a wheelchair. We say our goodbyes and thank them for taking care of me this past month.

"I better not see you here again," Nurse Hazel says with a smile.

"I'll try my best," I say.

KongKong parks his Toyota at the hospital entrance where Mom wheels me out. I stand up from the wheelchair on my own and go to greet my grandparents with a hug.

They help me into the minivan while Mom returns the wheelchair.

Once we're all settled in with seatbelts on, the minivan's engine comes to life and rumbles as KongKong drives off.

As the hospital fades from the window's view, I rip the identification band off my wrist and smile.

Daytime Monsters

October 25, 2017

"Ay-zuh-thi-o-prin."

I bring the prescription closer to my face. The white paper bag crinkles in my other hand. I squint and try again.

"Azathioprine," I say. The word flows out smooth this time.

Trees and buildings blur together outside the car window as Mom drives from the pharmacy to Guama and KongKong's place nearby. The leaves glitter in the sun's gold. A single contrail lines the clear sky. Cool air from the window's small gap lightly lifts my baby hairs.

Azathioprine is the new immunosuppressant that my rheumatologist prescribed for me. Even with all the other pills I shove down daily, my blood tests still don't show the greatest results.

But they were good enough to get me out of the hospital.

"Tsk. I don't like you taking all this medication," Mom says through clenched teeth. "But I know there's nothing else we can do right now." She tightens her grip on the steering wheel and focuses straight ahead on the road through dark Maui Jim sunglasses.

"Me neither," I say.

I lean on the Mazda's faded grey interior with my head turned toward the window until we round the familiar corner of old townhouses.

Mom pulls into the quiet neighbourhood and parks in front of unit twenty-two. The worn numbers hang on pale red bricks and under the brown roof's shade. We're greeted by an empty driveway and the front lawn's single tree.

I hop down from the car and up the stone steps. Instead of the doorbell, I reach for my phone to dial Chantel's number so she can let me in.

Waiting, I look down at the grooves between the cemented tiles to see if there are any potato bugs. When I was younger, I used to look for them there, even though they disgusted me.

The screen door creaks as Chantel pushes it open from the inside. From the car, Mom waves to

Chantel and gestures for me to come back before I go in.

"Are you going to be okay?" Mom says.

She keeps the engine running. It's a weekday, and she needs to go back to work. How much more can I ask of her after she had stayed with me every single day in the hospital for a whole month?

"I'll be fine, don't worry," I say. "Chant's with me."

"Okay, but if anything happens just call me, and I'll leave work right away. If they have a problem with that, they can just fire me," Mom says. She smirks, but I know she's serious.

"It'll be okay. See you later and drive safe."

I head inside and watch her car drive down the road until it's out of view. The bells around the knob jingle as I shut the door.

"Hey, what happened at the appointment today? Is everything okay?" Chantel says.

"Yeah, they just prescribed me a new immunosuppressant. The doctor said this one is stronger, and some people don't react well to it. If that happens, I'm supposed to stop taking it and call them."

I slip my shoes off at the entrance and slide on the wooden parquet floor with my socks to the living room. Everything's the same from a month ago when the ambulance took me to the hospital and from how I've remembered it these past few years – the piano hidden under red velvet covering, the decorative Chinese wall panels, the adjacent black sofas, the red lights of a prayer shrine above the flat screen TV, and the long blinds covering the back windows.

Wherever I am, it's always been home.

I flip the white paper bag and drop the azathioprine into my palm. The fifty-milligram pills rattle inside the transparent green container when I shake it to show Chantel.

I plop down onto KongKong's big maroon office chair beside the glass table and open my laptop so I can watch a show while I eat.

From the kitchen, Chantel brings me a glass of water and a steaming bowl of *makut* – pork bone soup – that Guama prepared earlier.

I wolf down the bowl before it has a chance to cool. The soup slides down my throat, dragging its heat with it. Tender meat slips off and reveals a clean bone.

Most people like to eat the rice on the side, but I dump it in my soup and eat it all together. It's been so long since I've had this dish; it's one of my favourites.

With a full meal in my stomach, I pop open the green container and drop two yellow pills of azathioprine into my palm.

Gulp. I take one at a time with a swig of water in between each.

Gulp. At least it's tasteless, unlike prednisone, which leaves an awful, bitter taste if it lingers on the tongue for even a second.

Click! I close the container and put it aside.

To pass the time, I re-watch episodes of *Noragami.* My fingers slide around my laptop's trackpad to exit out of three ads that pop up before the show can play. *I'm not looking for single women in my area, thank you very much.*

But I only last three episodes. I hit pause. My face twists with the slow knot of my insides. Pain invades my stomach; fear invades my mind. I bring my knees to my chest and wrap my arms around them.

"Chant?"

Her footsteps are swift, but heavy, as she runs down the stairs.

"Yeah?" Chantel says. But I just stare at her. "What's wrong?"

"I'm not sure," I say. "My stomach's hurting a bit."

"Is it the medicine?"

I shrug and look down at my stomach. It's not a wrenching pain, but my mind goes to the worst conclusions. I squeeze my knees tighter and let out a shaky breath that almost gives way to what would've been either a laugh or a cry. But either way, both would've been hysteric.

My mind seizes this daytime opportunity to release its monsters. And they come out with full force.

It probably is the medicine. Of course my body would fail me again. Nothing ever goes right.

"Maybe we should call Mom," Chantel says. The home phone glows orange as she dials Mom's work number. She hands it to me when Mom picks up.

"Hey, what's wrong?" Mom's voice is quiet so that her co-workers don't hear.

"I-I don't know. My stomach hurts," I say.

"What?" Mom says, much louder this time. "Is it the medicine?"

"I don't know … I don't know what's wrong."

I bite my lip to stop the quiver in my voice. But sobs reach her end of the phone instead. I can't seem to stop.

"Hold on, I'm leaving work. I'll be there soon," Mom says.

Selfish. You're causing problems again. What's wrong with you?

She hangs up, and I drop the phone to my lap. The dial tone stretches on in a duet with my cries. Chantel rubs my back as I bury my face in my hands.

"Why is there always something wrong with me?" I say.

My muffled words break up between sniffles, but she still hears me.

Here Again

November 20, 2018

"You okay?"

Mom hooks her arm with mine as we step through the doors of Mississauga Hospital. The warm tones of the morning sun turn to cold, white lights.

"I'll be okay," I say.

I give her arm a squeeze and smile. But that smile fades as we walk through the all-too-familiar halls that stretch on in front of us.

Following the signs above and the arrows below, we take the same path as always to Diagnostic Imaging.

I gaze at Mom's white hairs that her dyed dark brown hair can no longer hide.

It's been over a year since my one-month stay at the hospital, and today, I'm back for a kidney biopsy.

My new rheumatologist, Dr. Luca, was concerned about the results of my latest blood tests, with my protein count rising to around seven times more than it should be.

But the thought of another procedure grips me with the same fear from a year ago.

I look around at the empty chairs that fill the waiting room. No one wants to be here, especially in the early morning. I fiddle with my green health card and check the expiry date for when I can replace this mugshot.

The only good thing about today is that it's not a long wait, and soon, I'm signing in.

I hold out my wrist, prepared for them to tie the green and white identification band that reads "TENG, DANICA CHAR."

My full name doesn't fit. I think back to last year's stay; I remember wishing I could add "IZARD" at the end to make it Charizard, like the Pokémon.

Upon hearing my name, a staff member leads me to the dressing room and hands me a pale blue hospital gown. I stand alone in the stall no bigger than a broom closet. Unlike my first few hospital visits, I don't fumble around with the gown this time, putting it on quickly and tying the string of the open back.

A chatty, middle-aged woman with short blonde hair guides us to a different part of the hospital. A row of empty beds lines the room. The woman introduces a younger nurse who smiles at me.

"You're our youngest patient yet," the nurse says, guiding us to a bed near the end of the room.

I let out a faint laugh, but my heart twists at the unwanted achievement.

Mom helps me onto the bed, and my body sinks into the familiar mattress. The nurse leaves to get a needle for the IV, a part that makes me as nervous as the biopsy itself. Mom sits next to me and holds my hand.

"Youngest patient." Mom repeats the nurse's words, letting out a sigh. "I wish it weren't like this. I wish it were me instead."

I've heard Mom say this over and over, but it still hurts every time. She doesn't know that if this had to happen to someone in my family, I'm glad it was me. She doesn't know that without her, we would fall apart.

The nurse returns and tries to distract me with casual conversation as she gets the needle ready.

"How old are you?" She slips a new needle out of its packaging.

"I'm twenty years old," I say.

"Oh, you're the same age as my eldest child." She takes a sanitary wipe to my arm.

Here comes the furrowed brows and tilted head. It's the same look on every nurse who needs to draw blood from me. My veins are small and hard to find. The bruises from last year are permanently painted on my right arm. A stain on my skin. Sometimes, it takes up to four tries to draw some blood.

She settles for a place on my left hand instead and puts the needle in. My eyes squeeze shut.

"Sorry," the nurse says. She puts her hand over mine. A mother's touch.

The nurse tells us to wait here. After a while, a transporter – a staff member who brings patients around the hospital – comes to take me for the biopsy.

He wheels the bed I'm on, while Mom follows beside, through a lobby filled with people.

I clench the blanket and stare straight ahead, avoiding the eyes that I know are on me.

We turn a corner into a hallway filled with elderly people on beds, waiting for an operation, with relatives at their sides. I can feel all their eyes on me too. The youngest patient there. Getting me through the hall takes some maneuvering, but we finally make it to our destination.

A doctor with long, dark hair enters the room and introduces herself as Dr. Lee. She also introduces a younger medical student from the University of Toronto who watches.

Dr. Lee explains the procedure, telling me that they're going to use an ultrasound to guide the biopsy. After freezing my back with an anesthetic, they'll take out small samples from my kidney.

"Just so you know, you might hear a noise like *click!* Like a stapler," Dr. Lee says. "But don't worry about that, it's just the clamp."

I clench the blanket even harder. The thin layer isn't enough to protect my flesh from my own nails that dig in.

Time to start.

Shivers run down my bare back as they untie the gown's string. I feel a slight pinch from the anesthetic needle, then no pain after that. But even though I can't feel it, I can hear it. I grip the bedsheet in my fists as I lie on my stomach. *Click!*

"Do you feel any pain?" Dr. Lee asks.

"No, I'm okay," I say.

Click! I squeeze my eyes shut. Curiosity takes over, and I turn my head to the screen. The ultrasound shows a long stick protruding from my back.

Click! I plant my head back down into the bed. *Why the hell did I look?*

My eyes turn to Mom instead. She waits in the corner of the room. Her arms hug her body as she watches. For every procedure, even when non-hospital staff aren't supposed to be there, Mom asks the doctors if she can stay in the room. Sometimes, they give in.

Each click twists my stomach, but soon the biopsy is done. I can't feel the lower right side of my back, just the chill from the rest of my body. A transporter wheels me back to the room from where I came, except now, patients fill the row of beds.

"You should rest for the next two or three days, and no excessive exercise for the next week," a nurse says. She hands me a post-biopsy information sheet.

Mom sits next to the bed and feeds me as I lie down slightly upright. I'm not allowed to sit up straight. I'm not allowed to leave for the next few hours.

I try to make myself comfortable until I can go home tonight. I slept here for a month before. I can do it for one more day.

Sorry

November 24, 2018

Wilson's hand squeezes mine as we sit next to each other on the shuttle bus to Toronto. His dark hair falls over to the right, and the longer strands peek out over his forehead. He raises his thick brows and pulls his lips slightly inward.

"Are you gonna be okay?" he asks.

"Mhm, don't worry. I'll tell you if I need to rest," I say.

He plants a kiss on my head, and we continue listening to music on the bumpy ride.

The wired earphones, one for each of us, play Epik High's "Home Is Far Away." Conversations on the bus tune out as we raise the soft song's volume.

Tonight, we're going as part of Wilson's belated birthday celebration to Toronto's Cavalcade of Lights for their fireworks display. We'll also get to see our friend Alice, and I'll meet his cousin Mel and her boyfriend Ray who are visiting from Australia.

Prominent eye bags droop above my cheeks. It was another sleepless night despite my exhaustion.

It's been only four days since my kidney biopsy, but I didn't want to miss the lights. I couldn't go last year. And I'm still mad I missed the world's largest rubber duck too.

The post-biopsy instructions said I only had to rest for twenty-four to forty-eight hours. So, it should be fine.

I want to be here. I squeeze Wilson's hand tighter. *I want to be okay.*

By the time we arrive downtown, all the city's lights are on and brighten up the gloomy sky. Downtown Toronto at night both scares and fascinates me.

There's a slight drizzle as we walk through the streets, and I pull my hood over my head. Grit slides under our shoes as we tread on the glossy sidewalk for thirteen minutes following Google Maps to Cuppa Tea, where we're supposed to meet everyone else.

Wilson calls Alice's name when get there, and his deep voice booms in the quiet café. Alice already sits at a table near the front with a bubble tea, and I go to greet her with a hug. Her straight black hair falls against the back of her white turtleneck sweater. My eyesight's gotten worse. I didn't recognize her right away.

I slip out of my jacket before settling in a chair across from her. The wind made my hair wild, and my nose is rosy from the cold. But I'm not tired. *Still okay.*

We look over the choices on the menu. I order their Hong Kong style milk tea because it's their specialty. And because it comes in a cute glass bottle I get to keep. Wilson orders the same, along with a *bo lo bao* – pineapple bun.

The entrance door swings open, and Wilson waves to Mel and Ray. It's so easy to talk to them even though we've just met. So sociable. Just like Wilson.

The night grows darker as we get carried away with our conversations and drinks. The milk tea's sweet taste flows over my tongue. The buttery aroma of the piping hot pineapple bun surrounds our table.

"Oh shoot, what time is the event supposed to start?" I say.

"I think fireworks start at 8:30 p.m.," Alice says.

"Oops, we should probably get going. It's almost time already," Mel says.

Our chairs scrape against the floor as we get up. From Cuppa Tea, we head out toward Nathan Phillips Square. The rain persists, growing from a drizzle. I checked the estimated distance yesterday. Google said it's a sixteen-minute walk.

Boom! A loud crackling noise echoes through the night sky.

"I'm gonna take a wild guess and say the fireworks started," I say.

"Errr, maybe," Wilson says.

The buildings surround and tower over us, blocking our view of any breathtaking lights above.

By the time we get there, the fireworks are over. *Third time's the charm?* I cross my fingers for next year. There will be a next year, right?

But the music still plays. And the crowd's still here. We stand huddled in an empty spot and admire the giant Christmas tree set up near the festive ice rink with lights strung overhead.

I raise my phone to take a photo of the tree, and Wilson jumps in. I laugh and snap the shot, but he moves, leaving a slight blur.

"Thanks for giving me my new lock screen for the holidays," I say.

"Oh god." He laughs, his smile as bright as the tree.

“Sucks we missed the lights,” I say. “Maybe next time.”

“Should we go and get some dinner instead?” Ray asks.

“Yeah, dinner sounds good,” Wilson says. “Where do you guys want to eat?”

“We can probably walk toward the station and stop by some place on the way,” Alice says.

“If it gets too late, you guys can always stay at our place. We live nearby,” Mel says.

“That’d be nice. I think we’re good though,” Wilson says. “We should still have enough time before the last shuttle.”

“Plus, my mom might kill me,” I say with a chuckle.

We walk in two rows along Dundas Street as the wind pushes against us. Restaurants and bubble tea joints line the street. On a Saturday night, most of these places are either closed or packed with customers. Everywhere we look seems to be full. We approach Dagu Rice Noodle; its bright lights and savoury aroma leak outside, pulling us closer.

“Do you guys wanna eat here?” Mel asks.

“We’ve tried it before, it’s pretty good,” Ray says.

My eyes trace over people from the crowd inside to the lineup that goes outside their doors.

“Sure, I’m cool with eating anywhere,” I say.

Everyone else agrees on Dagu Rice Noodle. Ray goes in to put his name down on a list and comes back out to the cold. "They said it might be a twenty-minute wait," he says.

Wilson turns to me. "Are you gonna be okay?" he asks.

"I think so," I say, giving a smile.

And I really do. But then it happens. Again. Each exhale starts to feel heavy. The slow creep of fatigue gains on me each minute we spend standing outside. I crouch on the concrete as the dizziness slowly seeps in. The cold numbs my fingers and toes. My body slumps. The ground looks welcoming. Legs ready to collapse. Wilson knits his brows as he stares at me.

"You feeling okay?" Wilson asks.

"Kinda bleh," I say, closing my eyes. "Getting tired, I think."

"Mmm, a bit of space opened up inside. Let's wait there," Wilson says. He helps me up, then turns to everyone else. "Is it cool if we go inside first?"

They all nod, and I assure them I'm alright before going in.

We wiggle past people as Wilson leads me through the doorway. In the small foyer, two girls around our age sit on high white chairs while they wait for their tables.

"Here, let me ask them if–" Wilson heads to their direction, but I pull him back by his sleeve.

"No, don't. I'll be okay," I say.

I close my eyes to keep my head from spinning. *How much longer?*

"I'll ask the waiters if you can sit inside then," he says.

"No, don't worry. I–"

Those brown eyes, so dark they're almost black, give a piercing look that stops me.

"Let's go, I'll ask," he says.

I follow Wilson through the second set of doors. He signals to one of the waitresses.

"Hey, is there somewhere my girlfriend can sit? She just had a kidney biopsy recently so she can't stand for too long," he says.

"Oh, of course," the waitress says. Her eyes widen when she sees what a mess I am. "Right here."

She leads me to a chair in the corner by the door, which offers relief, until I feel the weariness I've tried to suppress.

Pain jolts through my body as I sit. I shrug off my jacket. Sweat drips down my face and covers my body. But the freezing air from outside still reaches me, and I put my jacket back on. The mix of hot and cold sticks to me like an extra layer and turns my stomach, urging me to throw up.

The desperation to stay awake overcomes everything else as I dread the thought of dragging everyone to a hospital with me. But at least there are hospitals all around this area. A last resort.

I inhale and exhale slowly, keeping my eyes closed, until we finally get a table.

I sit squished in between Mel and Alice. Wilson and Ray sit across from us. I let them order for me and close my eyes again. If I do anything, that urge to vomit nags me. The others keep asking if I'm okay. I keep responding with a nod and a smile.

Extravagant trays of separate ingredients paired with bowls of hot broth arrive at our table. I scoop some soup in my spoon, blowing on it twice first. I'm not sure what they ordered, but I can barely taste it. The heat warms me for a moment, but every sense I have left barely hangs on. I know it must be good. Everyone seems to enjoy it.

My stomach gives me a warning, and with no appetite, I only take a few more sips before I give the rest to Wilson.

As everyone eats, I take that time to rest. Unlike me, they're not such slow eaters, but we leave as the restaurant starts to close.

We step back out into darkness, protected by shining restaurant signs and dim streetlamps. But this time, my body feels a bit lighter, and my dizziness has died down.

"Is it okay if we actually do sleep at your place tonight?" Wilson asks Mel and Ray. "The last shuttle left already. I think we'd have to take the GO bus."

"Of course," Mel says, her cheerful smile is welcoming.

"Thanks. That's probably a good idea," I say. "I don't think I can walk back to Union Station."

I give a quick call to Mom explaining my situation. Knowing that I'm worrying her hurts worse than my stomach. But I reassure her that I'm fine. And she reassures me that she'll always allow it if it's the safest option for me. I thank her, say good night, and end the call.

The rain stops as we near the bus stations, and we say goodbye to Alice as she heads toward the TTC to go home. Wilson and I walk with Mel and Ray as they lead the way to their apartment close by. A five-minute walk.

After a short tour and time to relax with a hot cup of tea, we all go to bed. But even then, my thoughts don't let me sleep.

—

Grogginess still clings to me the morning after. We thank Mel and Ray for letting us stay, then head home.

But as if the night's events were still haunting me, we step out the door to find that one elevator at Mel and Ray's building is out of order. We wait. And wait more. The other one doesn't seem to be coming toward the fourteenth floor anytime soon. We drag our feet down the stairs, but after a few floors, I stop.

Mid-way, we decide to try the elevators again. When the silver doors part in the middle, the sight eases my whole body and I fling myself inside.

Sunshine showers us as we leave the building. Wilson and I walk toward the University of Toronto's St. George campus so we can take the shuttle back to the Mississauga campus. The weakness I feel still won't leave, and I suggest taking an Uber to campus instead. The old shuttle bus marks my goal line, and I hang my head down in relief as we plop down on the worn, grey seats.

"How're you feeling now?" Wilson says.

"So so," I say, slightly rocking my hand. "I think I'm *actually* okay now, as long as I don't move for a while. Thanks for taking care of me by the way. And I'm sorry …"

"What? No, don't worry," he says. "You don't need to say sorry."

But I do. I look down and bite my lip. Worry's been frozen on Wilson's expression since yesterday, even when he was trying to lighten the mood with jokes. *I'm sorry.* I want to say those words over and over.

Moving Forward

December 28, 2019

The uphill ahead of us stretches far beyond what Mom, Justin, and I can see. It's freezing in Montréal, making the trek even more challenging.

Living in Canada my whole life hasn't made dealing with winter any easier, and the arthritis I developed from lupus doesn't help either.

"We have to go all the way up there?" I say. My face scrunches as I turn to Justin and swing my finger toward Mount Royal – a hill from which the city takes its name.

"Yup, that's where we're headed," Justin says. His nose is red, and he tucks his hands into his pockets. "I went up there during the summer. Let's go, you guys will love the view."

But Mom and I slouch our shoulders when we look at the endless sidewalk that we have to endure just to get to the base of the hill.

From there, it's stairs and more stairs all the way up.

"Make sure you bundle up," Mom says.

I zip up my black jacket all the way, squishing my grey scarf closer so it hugs my neck. From my pocket, I pull the red plaid ski mittens Mom made me bring last minute and wear them over the thin red gloves that I originally packed.

Staring at the summit, I wonder if it's too late to run back to our hotel room. I bite my lip as we start moving forward. *In and out.*

In twenty-one years, this is my second time traveling outside my home of Ontario. Just eight months earlier, I went to Vancouver. I'm more stable now. I can do this. While I'm here, I want to explore everything.

The wind pushes against us as we walk up past the busy street on our left and the diagonal slope of crooked houses on our right. A breeze blasts our faces with cold air, which lingers on the gold frame of my glasses and pushes back my faux-fur hood.

By the time we make it to the base of the hill, I can feel the fatigue shadowing each step, waiting for its chance to take over.

"Don't forget to tell us if you need a break, okay?" Mom says.

"Will do," I say. And this time, I mean it.

We pause to take in the journey ahead. Behind us, the bustling city ends and gives way to nature. A veil of trees surrounds the area, and frost clings to their bare branches.

On ice-covered grounds, the scattered pools of dry mud are the only safe spots. All the paths are frozen, leaving nothing but the rough mass of trees to hold onto until you reach the wooden stairs that lead to the top.

Tourists roam the area, and we watch as people struggle in their running shoes or winter boots to skate back down the hill. As they slip and slide on the ice, nervous laughter escapes the three of us as we've just seen our future coming back.

Some people manage to tread slowly and reach safe grounds, while others involuntarily take the fast way down.

Mom and I lock arms while we walk so that neither of us fall. Justin takes the lead, filming our hike on his phone. The phone stabilizer he bought makes all our vacation videos look professional.

When we reach the platform after the first flight of stairs, I'm already out of breath. But I'm not surprised.

"Hold up," I say. "Give me a minute."

I lean on the railing to the side, letting people pass by as I crouch to rest. Mom and Justin hang back to wait till I'm ready to move again. I take a few deep breaths – in and out – and stand up.

"Okay, I'm ready," I say.

"You sure?" Justin asks.

"Yeah, but I'll probably have to stop again soon."

And we do, after the second flight of stairs. Once we reach the next platform, I crouch again.

As they wait for me, Mom and Justin take pictures of the view behind us. I rest my head on my knees, looking at my boots on the wooden planks speckled with dirt and gravel. Sweat sticks to my face. The conflicting mix of hot and cold makes me squirm.

We move forward again, and I continue stopping to rest every few minutes. Justin turns back with his camera lens pointed at us. The wind's pushed strands of my bangs in different directions. My glasses rest unevenly on my flushed face. I walk, drunk with fatigue, up the steps to the next platform.

Looking up at the flights of stairs that remain, my head tilts back as I let out a groan.

"How much farther?" I ask. I crouch behind Justin's tall figure and use him as a shade from the sun.

"I think we're about halfway there," Justin says.

"Only half? Are you kidding?"

"Are you going to be okay?" Mom says.

"Uhhh, well, I can't go back down now. Might as well go all the way up," I say.

Either way, it'll be tiring. It's cold. My feet ache. The more stairs we climb, the more I want to lie down.

But as I raise my hand to my forehead, squinting against the bright sunlight, I see the top of the hill in the distance marked by a chalet.

The goal is in sight. *In and out.* I move forward.

After the arduous climb up, step by step, we reach the top of Mount Royal.

Crowds line the guarded edge where the view awaits us. But the chalet comes first. If I don't sit down soon, I might just pass out.

We head inside first and manage to find a small table. I drop on the chair and rest my head against the table's cool surface. I close my eyes and sit still, taking deep breaths. Nausea swirls in my stomach. I hear laughter and conversations all around me.

"Don't look outside the window yet. Wait till you go out first to see the view," Justin says.

"If we're resting here for now, is there anything hot to drink?" Mom asks.

"Yeah, there should be. Wait here. I'll see if they have some tea."

Without lifting my head, I raise a thumbs-up. After my dizziness starts to clear, I open my eyes to see Mom taking pictures.

The chalet's ceiling is covered in russet arches adorned with sculptures of squirrels. Multiple chandeliers that carry their bulbs in dumb-bell-shaped fixtures line the middle. Framed art pieces hang on the walls, and the glass doors that surround the chalet let in plenty of natural light. Children run to the gift shop, and parents line up to order food.

Justin comes back with Styrofoam cups of steaming green tea and hands one to me and one to Mom.

"Thanks," I say, letting the cup warm my hands.

"None for you?" Mom asks Justin.

"Nah, I'm good," Justin says. "Lemme know when you guys are ready."

I blow on my tea, leaving ripples on the surface. I try a small sip first, then take a bigger gulp once I'm sure it's cooled down enough to spare my tongue. The tea's heat comforts my aching body.

After resting a bit longer and checking out the gift shop, we brace ourselves to go back outside.

When we step out, the ground's less icy, but we're still careful and take each step with caution on our way down the stone steps. Everyone at the edge either takes pictures, looks at the view, or does both at the same time. We wait for a space to clear in the swarm and sneak in when we get the chance.

I place both hands on the railing and look straight ahead. The view before me overlooks the city of Montréal.

A sea of buildings, both new and old, sits below a light blue gradient of clear sky. You can see water and bridges beyond, and the land starts to fade past that. Even farther, more hills lay hidden in fog.

A cool breeze washes over me as I take in the vast scene. A chill runs through me. There's so much to see. I inhale all the fresh air I can and exhale everything away.

Epilogue

I've always kept these stories, or at least my versions of them, to myself. But it's freeing to be able to finally share them.

In the earliest drafts of this compilation, the summed-up version of what one of my writing professors told me was:

"Why do you always make it seem like everything's okay?"

At first, I didn't understand.

It was only later during my revision of these stories that I realized perhaps he knew I wasn't being honest with myself, even before I knew it.

Though I documented my struggles, I always ended on a positive note that wasn't entirely true to what I felt. Maybe it was only how I wanted to feel.

The hope within my stories wasn't a bad thing, but the problem was that it dismissed the dark reality.

There needs to be a balance.

Even outside of writing, I have a habit of treating my lupus like it's no big deal. But that's wrong. Lupus is difficult and terrifying, engulfing me in the worst kinds of pain.

However, while it may have changed a part of me, my life does not belong to lupus. Bringing back balance, these experiences made me realize a lot about myself and have shown me I have an amazing support system of people who love me. It's because of them and my own strength that I'm able to get through this life with lupus.

I'm sure I'll still have a lot more stories to tell in the future. There will be some happy endings, and some bad ones, but I can live with that.

Acknowledgements

To Mom, thank you for always staying with me. I hope that one day I can be even half as strong and hardworking as you are. There will never be enough words to express how much I love you.

To Chantel and Justin, thank you for always taking care of your little sister, even as she grows more chaotic by the day. Your influences have helped shape the person I am today.

To KongKong and Guama, thank you for always being there for me and for the warmth of a home I can always go back to. You both believed I'd be an author, even before I did. Mahal na mahal ko po kayong dalawa.

To Wilson, thank you for all your love and constant reassurance through tough times. You show me life's craziness and make each day one to look forward to.

To my family and friends, thank you for being in my life and for the endless support. You've all helped me out of darkness more times than you know.

To Katherine, my editor, I couldn't be happier to have a familiar face working with me. Thank you for letting me share my story with you and for helping me tell it.

To Jenefer, Vanessa, and Kriti, thank you for all your kind words and for keeping me sane throughout the book making process. I couldn't have asked for a better editing group.

To everyone in the healthcare industry who has taken care of me, thank you for helping me on my road to recovery.

To all my PWC professors, Guy Allen, Robert Price, Laurel Waterman, John Currie, Joshua Dittrich, Rahul Sethi, and Nicole Cohen, thank you for your guidance and for nurturing my love of writing. You've given me every confidence to continue to write. These are lessons I'll never forget.

Special thanks to my first PWC professor, Robert Price, who guided me during *Chrysalis*'s beginnings, and to my last professor, Guy Allen, who helped see it through to the very end.

About the Author

Danica Ong Teng studied in the Professional Writing & Communication program and the English program at the University of Toronto Mississauga. During her time at university, she has written articles for The Medium's Arts section. Her short story, "The Girl in the Mirror," will also be published in UTM Scribes' *Slate: Volume VI.*

Danica is a lupus patient fuelled by milk tea, and you can usually find her pulling out her hair trying to write or sleeping as she dreams of having her own Studio Ghibli adventure.

Manufactured by Amazon.ca
Bolton, ON

33937675R00076